Brer Rabbit
and the
Blackberry Bush

Retold by Louie Stowell

Illustrated by
Eva Muszynski

Reading Consultant: Alison Kelly
Roehampton University

This is a story about
Brer Rabbit,

Brer Fox

and a prickly
blackberry bush.

Brer Rabbit and Brer Fox were enemies.

One day, Brer Fox
set a trap.

and wriggled...

...but he
was stuck.

"Got you!"
growled Brer Fox.

"Now I'm going to eat
you all up!"

"Hurray!"
said Brer Rabbit.

"Do you *want* to be eaten?" asked Brer Fox.

"Oh yes," said Brer Rabbit. "Fry me...

boil
me...

...eat me in
a pie!"

"But please..."

"Don't throw me in the
blackberry bush!"

He picked up Brer Rabbit.

Then he threw him through the air.

Brer Rabbit landed...

...right in the middle of the blackberry bush.

THWUMP!

Brer Rabbit
laughed.

He ran deeper into
the dark and prickly
blackberry bush.

I was born in
the blackberry bush!

Brer Fox growled.

He couldn't get
Brer Rabbit.

PUZZLES

Puzzle 1

Put the pictures in order.

A

B

C

D

E

F

Puzzle 2
Choose the best sentence in each picture.

A

B

Puzzle 3

Can you spot the differences between these two pictures?

There are six
to find.

Puzzle 4
Find these things in the picture:

birds   rabbit

caterpillar   blackberry bush

fox

Answers to puzzles

Puzzle 1

D   F   A

B   E   C

Puzzle 2

A   B

"I am angry."   "We're enemies."

Puzzle 3

Puzzle 4

rabbit

fox

birds

caterpillar

blackberry bush

About this story

In the 19th century, an American named Joel Chandler Harris wrote a series of tales about Brer Rabbit, Brer Fox, and other animal characters. But he didn't entirely make them up. A lot of his stories are very similar to earlier African and Cherokee legends.

Designed by Caroline Spatz
Series editor: Lesley Sims
Series designer: Russell Punter
Digital manipulation: John Russell

First published in 2008 by Usborne Publishing Ltd., Usborne House,
83-85 Saffron Hill, London EC1N 8RT, England. www.usborne.com
Copyright © 2008 Usborne Publishing Ltd.